The Prayers of President Trump

The Reverend Billy Tillich

Copyright © 2025 The Reverend Billy Tillich

All rights reserved.

ISBN: 979-8-3483-9338-0

DEDICATION

To the citizens of the United States of American, especially the believers who seek to make America great again.

CONTENTS

    Acknowledgments   i

1. Prayers for National Healing   Pg 1
   Prayer for National Healing
   Prayer for Comfort

2. Prayers to Make America Great Again   Pg 6
   Prayer to Make America Great Again
   Prayer for the Border
   Prayer to Drain the Swamp

3. Prayers for My Friends and Enemies   Pg 10
   Prayer for Mr. Putin
   Prayer for the Pope
   Prayer for Melania
   Prayer for Ivanka
   Prayer for Baron
   Prayer for Biden
   Prayer for Kamala
   Prayer for Obama
   Prayer for Pence
   Prayer for Nancy
   Prayer for Mitch

4. Prayers for the Nation   Pg 23
   Prayer for the U.S. Constitution
   Prayer for the U.S. Supreme Court

5. Prayers for Christian Values   Pg 26
   Prayer for Hope
   Prayer for Justice
   Prayer for Women
   Prayer for Men
   Prayer for the Nuclear Family Unit

    About the Author   Pg 53

ACKNOWLEDGMENTS

The President of the United States of America Donald J. Trump—our leader. May his prayers protect our Nation and change our world. God bless the United States of America.

CHAPTER 1

PRAYERS FOR NATIONAL HEALING

- *2 Chronicles 7:14:* "*If my people, which are called by my name, shall humble themselves, and pray, and seek my face, and turn from their wicked ways; then will I hear from heaven, and will forgive their sin, and will heal their land.*"
- *Psalms 147:3:* "*He healeth the broken in heart, and bindeth up their wounds.*"

Prayer for National Healing

O Father, God of our magnificent universe, and Lord of our majestic Nation:

We seek thy presence throughout our land, for our help and healing can only come through you.

We come as one community experiencing a common crisis, joined together as citizens of these United of America—one from many.

We, as a Nation, invite you to dwell among us, as you have been our dwelling place across the ages.

In all generations, you have been our provider and our healer.

In times of crisis, mourning, and sorrow, we seek your powerful hands to prop us up on all leaning sides and your shining face to guide us through the dark days of distress.

You are a God that can heal the broken-hearted and bind up their wounds.

As a Nation, we have experienced many wounds and have been near broken, but God you mended these United States together and saved our Union. As you have done it before, we ask you to do it again.

Help us, O' Lord, to face the difficult days ahead. Give us courage and strength to make it through the rough patches. Give us hope for brighter days, give us faith for the present day, and give us charity to love our neighbors.

We know, O God, that our Nation can be healed—be the glue

to our divisions, and the fasteners for our fractures. Heal us now, O, God—put us back to together again. Provide the healing and peace that will surpass all our understanding. Be our protector as we are restored in our greatness. Be our comforter as our hearts are heavy. Take away the grief that has befallen us. Let no tragedy derail our spirit of unity as we come together as One to render this prayer.

And now Lord, may your peace prevail as the Nation recovers and heals. As we put the pieces back together again, let us know you as a healer. We thank you God for this national healing. Into your hands, we place our hope and our healing and our future.

God bless these United States of America. Amen

Prayer for Comfort

Dear God, We come together today in need of comfort—heart- and soul-healing comfort. We are in the midst of tough and difficult times. And God, we turn to you now, more than ever, to give us strength and courage to sustain us.

God, you've been with us from the beginning, and we know you're with us now. You've blessed this great country, and we trust you will continue to guide us through whatever challenges come our way.

We ask you to comfort everyone who's hurting right now. To lift them up and remind them of the incredible power that lies within them. Give them peace, give them hope, and give them the faith that things will get better—because they will.

We know that with your help, there's nothing we can't do. We'll come out stronger, better, and more united than ever before. Thank you, God for the restoration that is on the way. We trust you. Amen.

CHAPTER 2

PRAYERS TO MAKE AMERICA GREAT AGAIN

Prayer to Make America Great Again

- *Psalms 71:21: God increases our greatness and comforts us.*

Eternal God, make America great again!

Restore our land to the promise of yesterday and prepare us for the prosperity of tomorrow.

Help us to remember our days of glory and great industry.

Help us to reclaim the days of old when law and order prevailed from coast to coast.

Help us to recall the nights that we could sleep without locking our front doors,

The cattle on a thousand hills in the north country and down in the plains of the lowlands belong to you!

The gold that runs like veins deep within the earth belong to you!

Our plentiful harvests that flow from farms to tables belong to you!

May the industrial machines that make us mighty keep on turning!

And then hold the conscience of the nation together connected by the godly values that treat every human being with respect and kindness.

Lord, make America great again—the home of the free and brave! Amen.

Prayer for the Border

- *2 Chronicles 32:5: Also he strengthened himself, and built up all the wall that was broken, and raised it up to the towers, and another wall without, and repaired Millo in the city of David, and made darts and shields in abundance.*

Lord, help up to repair and build up the walls; and secure our borders.

O God, give us the intelligence needed to create safety at every border.

Lord, they say that good fences make good neighbors.

Help us to maintain our border fences.

Like Nehemiah, help us to build and repair our walls so that our nation can be fortified against all manner of evil.

Help those who seek to cross where they are.

Help those who seek to cross understand that there is a right way and a wrong way.

Help us to defend those borders when they are threatened.

Give us the ability to do what we can to make our borders safe.

Amen.

Prayer to Drain the Swamp

Dear God,
We come before You today, and we ask for Your strength and wisdom. We know this country is the greatest in the world, but it's been held back for too long by corrupt politicians, swamp creatures, and special interests who don't care about the American people.

We need Your help, Lord, to clean up Washington, D.C. and drain the swamp once and for all. We need bold leaders who will fight for the people. We need accountability. We need transparency. We need to put America First – and that means getting rid of the people who have been stealing from us, lying to us, and putting their own interests above the American worker.

We ask for Your guidance to help expose the corruption, to restore integrity to our government, and to ensure that no one is above the law. Give us the courage to stand up and fight for what's right, even when it's tough. Let us put an end to the lies and deceit, and bring real change to Washington.

Lord, we know You have the power to make it happen. With Your strength, we can win this fight. Thank You for Your blessings, and for helping us bring honesty, fairness, and greatness back to our country.

In Your name,
Amen.

CHAPTER 3

PRAYERS FOR MY FRIENDS AND ENEMIES

Matthew 5:44 : But I say unto you, Love your enemies, bless them that curse you, do good to them that hate you, and pray for them which despitefully use you, and persecute you…

Matthew 5:44 : But I say unto you, Love your enemies, bless them that curse you, do good to them that hate you, and pray for them which despitefully use you, and persecute you…

Prayer for Putin

Dear Lord, I pray for my friends and my enemies.

I pray for President Putin. Let him come to know America as a friend.

There is a time for war, and a time for peace.

There is a time to tear apart, and a time to bring together.

There is a time be separate, and a time to be at the table together.

Let these years be fruitful between us. Let these years be productive.

Let us put the past behind us and look toward a brighter future.

Help him to know that together we are stronger and divided he is weak.

Give us a new understanding to forge new relations for our people and the world.

Amen.

Prayer for the Pope

Dear Lord, we thank you for the incredible work of Pope Francis. He's a tremendous leader, a man of faith, doing great things for the Church. He has a true heart for the people. We ask you to bless him, guide him, and give him the strength to continue leading with wisdom and courage. We know he has a tough job, but he's got what it takes, just like all the great leaders we've had. Keep him strong, keep him healthy, and keep him safe.

Lord, we also ask for your protection and your blessing on the entire Church. So many good people, doing good work, all over the world. We want them to be successful, to spread peace, and to be united. It's a beautiful thing, really. Together, we'll make sure we continue to make the world better, more peaceful, and more prosperous.

We thank you, Lord, for your guidance, and we ask that you continue to watch over the Pope. Keep him in your light, give him strength, and help him lead with love. Amen.

Prayer for Melania

Dear God, we come together today to give thanks for Melania, a truly incredible woman. She's been a tremendous First Lady, more elegant and more accomplished than anyone could have ever imagined. She's beautiful, strong, and has the heart of a lion.

We ask for your continued blessings on her, to guide her with wisdom, strength, and grace, as she always does so well. Her dedication to our country, to children, to people in need—it's really something special.

Please watch over her, protect her, and keep her healthy, safe, and surrounded by love. We know that with God's guidance, she will continue to be a great example for this Nation, a true role model.

Thank you, God, for giving us Melania. She's a true treasure, and we're so proud of her.

In Your name, Amen.

Prayer for Ivanka

God in Heaven, we come to you today, and we thank You for Ivanka—she's a wonderful woman, truly wonderful. A great daughter, a great leader, a great businesswoman. She's been with me through so much, and she's always shown strength and intelligence.

We ask You, Lord, to continue blessing her with Your wisdom. She's a great friend to so many, always looking out for others, and we know that's what You want. So, give her strength in everything she does, and guide her path to continue making America proud. She's a true champion for all people.

Please protect her, watch over her, and let her continue to thrive in everything—she deserves it all. She's done so much for this country, and I know she will continue to do even more, bringing success, greatness, and prosperity to the people. You've blessed us with her, and we thank You.

In Your name, Amen.

Prayer for Baron

Dear God, we come before You today with gratitude, and we thank You for the incredible blessing that is my son, Baron. What a tremendous young man he is—smart, strong, and just a tremendous guy. Baron, as you know, has always been such a great kid. He's a winner and he's going to do amazing things.

So, I ask You today, God, to watch over Baron. Protect him, guide him, and help him grow stronger every day. Give him the wisdom to make the best decisions and the strength to face any challenges that come his way. We know he's got the talent, but we ask You, Lord, to continue to bless him with Your grace.

We also thank You for the love and support we get from this great country, and for all the great people who care about our family. We've got the best people, folks, you know that. Baron's future is bright, so we trust in You, God, to help him succeed in all that he does.

Thank You, Lord, for giving us such a wonderful son. We're so proud of him, and with Your help, he'll continue to make us proud.

Amen.

Prayer for President Joe Biden

Dear God, we come to You today, to pray for our great Nation, and for Joe Biden, our current President. We all know Joe's been through a lot, and it's not easy--not easy at all. But we pray, with all our hearts, that You give him the strength, the wisdom, and the courage to lead this country—this amazing country—forward.

America is the greatest country in the world, and no one's going to beat us, we know that. But we need leadership. And we ask You, God, to guide President Biden during his last few days—help him make the right decisions in his final hours, help him stay strong, and, frankly, make America great again. Because that's what we all want. We want strength, we want prosperity, and we want safety. We want our military to be the best, we want our economy to be booming, and we want our borders to be secure. We all know that's what America needs.

God, we ask for Your guidance for Joe. Let him make good, smart decisions—decisions that make America stronger, safer, and more respected around the world. Help him bring people together, help him heal divisions. And then, God, we thank him for his service and help me repair the Nation following his term.

And of course, God, protect this country, protect our people, protect our great troops, and keep us strong. We trust in You, and we know You've got a plan for this country.

Amen.

Prayer for Kamala

Dear God, we come together today to lift up Kamala, the Vice President of our great country. She's in a tough job, and we all know it. It's not easy being in the position she's in, especially after losing a national election. Help her to heal. But we trust in your guidance, because, let me tell you, nobody knows better than you.

We ask for wisdom, strength, and clarity for Kamala. She's got a lot of decisions to make, and it's critical that she makes the right ones. We need strong leadership, and we pray she gets that strength from you, the ultimate source. She's got a big responsibility – probably the biggest – and she needs your help, Lord.

Give her the courage to do what's right for America, the people, the country that we all love. We're praying for her to have the clarity to put America First, just like we did. We need her to focus on winning for the American people, and that's what we pray for today.

In Your name, we pray. Amen.

Prayer for Barack Obama

Dear God, we come to You today, and I just want to say thank for great American leaders. We've had some great leaders, no doubt about it, and Barack Obama was one of them. A lot of people talk about him--some people say he did a great job, others, not so much, but we respect him. We really do.

So, today, we're praying for Barack. We pray for his health, for his family, and for the future, which—let me tell you—it's looking very bright. He's had his time, a lot of people remember that time, and we want to make sure he stays strong, stays healthy.

And Lord, we ask You to guide him. Give him wisdom, give him peace, give him strength. Because, as we all know, the job never ends. We know he's been working hard, just like all of us, and we ask You to bless him in everything he does going forward.

We ask You, God, to watch over him. Protect him, protect his family, and give him the guidance he needs. Because the world needs a lot of good people, and we know he's one of the good ones.

In Your name, we pray. Amen.

Prayer for Mike Pence

Dear Lord, we come to you today to lift up Mike—forgive him for he knew not what he was doing. Help me to forgive him as I know that you have already forgiven him. Create in him a clean heart. He's a man of tremendous faith, and we know you've guided him in so many ways. We ask you, Lord, to continue to give him wisdom, strength, and protection as he walks the path you've laid out for him.

Mike, as we know, always tries to put America first. He's done tremendous work for our country, and we're proud of his legislative career. We thank him for his service.

So, we ask you, Lord, to bless Mike, to give him the vision and courage to continue doing great things for this Nation. Keep him safe, keep him strong, and keep him focused on what's best for America. We know you've got a plan for him.

In Your name, we pray. Amen.

Prayer for Nancy

Dear God, we pray for Nancy Pelosi. Now, you know, I've had some tough battles with Nancy, we've disagreed on a lot, but she's been there a long time—a very long time.

Dear God, we ask for Your guidance for Nancy Pelosi. We may not always see eye to eye, but You know what's best for all of us, and we trust in Your wisdom. Give Nancy the strength to do what's right for the country, for the American people, and guide her to make decisions that help us all. Rid her of all nastiness.

We know she's a tough lady, she's got a lot of energy, but we pray that she uses that energy for good, for unity, and for America's greatness. God bless her, and God bless the United States of America.

Amen.

Prayer for Mitch McConnell

Dear God, we come to You today with a special prayer for Mitch. He's been through a lot, folks, a LOT--tremendous things. but he's still standing strong, still leading, and many are so grateful for him.

Help Mitch to transition from Washington, D.C. to home. Help to him to know that his service has been appreciated. Help him to know that his term has limits.

We know You're watching over him, protecting him. We ask for Your guidance in the days ahead, to give Mitch the clarity and determination to continue making America great. We trust in You, God. Thank You.

Amen.

CHAPTER 4

PRAYERS FOR THE NATION

Prayer for the U.S. Constitution

God, we thank You for the greatest country in the world—America. We know the United States Constitution is one of the greatest documents ever written, truly a masterpiece. It was crafted by the best minds, our Founding Fathers, who created a system like no other, a system that's worked better than any other in the history of mankind.

We ask for Your blessing on our Constitution, to keep it strong and true, as we always have. It's a document of freedom—freedom that the world looks to. We want to protect it, we want to defend it. And we will always defend it.

Please help us to uphold the principles of liberty, of justice, and of freedom, as written in this great Constitution. Help us to always fight for it, fight for the American people. Help us to remember that America was built on values that will never go away—values that make us proud, that make us great, and that keep us winning.

We ask You to give our leaders the wisdom to protect this amazing document, to fight for it with everything we've got. We'll always protect the Constitution, because it's what makes us who we are—strong, free, and exceptional.

Thank You, God, for America. Thank You for our Constitution. We will continue to make America great, and we will always honor and protect the Constitution.

In Your name, Amen.

Prayer for the Supreme Court

Lord, justice belongs to you.

We give to you the United States Supreme Court.

Help them to deliver justice wisely.

Give them the understanding of the law and the knowledge to apply it.

Be with them as they interpret the law for the people.

Let them know that they are not makers of the law but keepers of the law.

Guide them to know right from wrong.

May your will be done through their opinions.

Amen.

CHAPTER 7

PRAYERS FOR CHRISTIAN VALUES

Prayer for Hope

Dear God,

We come together, as a nation, to ask for your guidance. We've been through tough times, believe me, the toughest. But we're strong, and we know that with your help, we can rise above anything. You've blessed this country before, and we know you can do it again.

Give us the strength to face each day, no matter how hard. Give us the wisdom to lead with courage, to make America strong again and even greater. We need hope, Lord. We need that American spirit – the best spirit – to keep us going.

Bless every family, every worker, every patriot who's fighting for a better future. You've given us so much, and we know with your blessing, there's nothing we can't do. We believe in this country, and we believe in you.

We trust that you'll bring us through this, stronger than ever. We thank you, Lord, for your love, your mercy, and your hope.

Amen.

Prayer for Justice

God, we come before You today, strong and proud, as we seek justice for our great nation. We know that justice is what makes America truly great. We've seen it before—when the right thing happens, when we stand together, when the truth is honored, this country soars like never before.

We ask You, Lord, to bring fairness, to bring accountability. We need justice—real justice—across this land. We need it in our courts, in our streets, in our communities. Everyone should be treated equally, no one above the law. We want peace, we want safety, we want security. And we know that true justice leads to all of that.

We thank You for the blessings You've given us, but we know we must continue to fight for what's right. Give us the strength to stand up for justice, to protect our freedoms, and to make sure that truth prevails. We trust You, God, because You are the ultimate judge, and with You, justice will always win.

In Your name, we pray. Amen.

Prayer for Men

God, we pray for the men of our nation--they're strong, they're hard-working, and they get things done. But, sometimes, even the strongest need help. So today, we're going to pray for all the great men out there – the fathers, the brothers, the sons, the workers, the leaders, the fighters.

We pray, Lord, for strength. Give them the courage to stand up for what's right. Nobody stands taller than a man who knows what's right, and we need more of that. More strength, more courage.

We pray, Lord, for wisdom. Men need wisdom to make the best decisions, to lead with vision. And we all know that vision makes the difference – it always has. Help them see clearly, Lord, and make choices that make America, and the world, a better place.

Keep them strong, Lord. Keep them on the path to greatness. And Lord, we pray for family. Men need to be great fathers, great husbands, great brothers. Family is what it's all about – they are the foundation. Help them be great in their homes, Lord, because when they're great there, they're great everywhere else too.

We thank You, Lord, for these men. They're truly incredible. We're blessed to have them, and we ask that You guide them with Your wisdom and Your grace.

In Your name, we pray. Amen.

Prayer for Women

Dear God, we thank you for the phenomenal, strong, and resilient women in this country. They are truly amazing—tough, smart, and full of potential. We've seen it all. Women are doing tremendous things. From the boardrooms to the military, from the family to the marketplace, they're leaders, they're winners, and we're proud of them.

We pray that you continue to bless them, keep them strong, protect them, and lift them up. They've got the power, God, the power to succeed, the power to lead, and the power to overcome any challenge that comes their way. Women have been vital to the success of this nation, and we'll never forget that. They are truly the backbone of our great country.

We ask for your guidance, for strength in times of struggle, and wisdom to make the right decisions. We know you're with them every step of the way, guiding them to greatness.

We believe in their greatness. We believe in American women. Together, we'll make this country even greater.

Thank you, God. Amen.

Prayer for the Great Nuclear Family Unit

Dear God – we all know that the nuclear family is the backbone of this country, the heart of America. We're praying for the nuclear family unit because it deserves it. Families are strong, they're powerful, they're the foundation of everything great that we've built.

We're asking for blessings. Protect these families, protect the moms, the dads, the kids – everyone. Keep them strong, keep them together. Because when families are strong, America is strong. No doubt about it.

We want peace in their homes. Peace and love--no one knows how to do it better than you do. We need the best guidance. The kind that helps families stay together, keep working hard, stay united. That's how we win, that's how we keep winning, generation after generation.

We thank God for the family, the real family. The one that raises kids, teaches them values, and makes this country great. We're not going to let anything break that bond. We're not going to let anything tear us apart, because we know the power of the family.

So let's pray together, for strength, for unity, and for the nuclear family. God bless them, and God bless America.

PRAYER JOURNAL

PRAYERS OF PRESIDENT TRUMP

PRAYERS OF PRESIDENT TRUMP

PRAYERS OF PRESIDENT TRUMP

PRAYERS OF PRESIDENT TRUMP

PRAYERS OF PRESIDENT TRUMP

PRAYERS OF PRESIDENT TRUMP

PRAYERS OF PRESIDENT TRUMP

PRAYERS OF PRESIDENT TRUMP

PRAYERS OF PRESIDENT TRUMP

PRAYERS OF PRESIDENT TRUMP

PRAYERS OF PRESIDENT TRUMP

PRAYERS OF PRESIDENT TRUMP

PRAYERS OF PRESIDENT TRUMP

PRAYERS OF PRESIDENT TRUMP

PRAYERS OF PRESIDENT TRUMP

PRAYERS OF PRESIDENT TRUMP

PRAYERS OF PRESIDENT TRUMP

ABOUT THE AUTHOR

The Reverend Billy Tillich is a Protestant theologian with decades of evangelistic witness of the Christian gospel. Rev. Tillich is a firm believer in the power of prayer. He believes that President Donald J. Trump will protect and defend the spiritual values of our nation.

www.prayersofpresidenttrump.com

Donate Today at the website above to assist this publication with operations!

www.ingramcontent.com/pod-product-compliance
Lightning Source LLC
LaVergne TN
LVHW042243070526
838201LV00088B/3